JUNIOR
BIOGRAPHY
FROM
ANCIENT
CIVILIZATIONS

NERO

PETE DIPRIMIO

Mitchell Lane
PUBLISHERS

P.O. Box 196
Hockessin, Delaware 19707
Visit us on the web: www.mitchelllane.com
Comments? Email us: mitchelllane@mitchelllane.com

JUNIOR BIOGRAPHY FROM
ANCIENT CIVILIZATIONS

**Alexander the Great • Archimedes
Augustus Caesar • Confucius • Genghis Khan
Homer • Leif Erikson • Marco Polo
Nero • Socrates**

ABOUT THE AUTHOR: Pete DiPrimio is an award-wining Indiana sportswriter, a long-time freelance writer, and a veteran children's author. He's also a journalism adjunct lecturer and fitness instructor.

PUBLISHER'S NOTE: The facts on which the story in this book is based have been thoroughly researched. Documentation of such research can be found on pages 44–45. While every possible effort has been made to ensure accuracy, the publisher will not assume liability for damages caused by inaccuracies in the data, and makes no warranty on the accuracy of the information contained herein.

Printing   1   2   3   4   5   6   7   8   9

Library of Congress
Cataloging-in-Publication Data

DiPrimio, Pete.
  Nero / by Pete DiPrimio.
    pages cm. — (Junior biography from ancient civilizations)
  Includes bibliographical references and index.
  ISBN 978-1-61228-439-2 (library bound)
  1. Nero, Emperor of Rome, 37–68—Juvenile literature. 2. Emperors—Rome—Biography—Juvenile literature. 3. Rome—History—Nero, 54-68. I. Title.
  DG285.D47 2013
  937'.07092—dc23
  [B]
                                    2013012560

eBook ISBN: 9781612285016
                                    PLB

CONTENTS

Phonetic pronunciations of words in **bold**
can be found on page 46.

Emperor Nero wears a laurel wreath crown in this painting by 17th Century Dutch artist Pieter Fransz de Grebber. In ancient Rome, such crowns were usually given to successful commanders and leaders after great victories.

CHAPTER 1
An Angry Emperor

Nero stabbed a grape with a knife, jammed it into his mouth, and chewed bitterly.

"The people hate me and the senate plots against me," the emperor said. "After all I have done, I don't deserve this."

Nero stood on a limestone balcony looking over Rome. A setting sun glowed fat and orange above the city's blackened ruins and new construction that stretched from the Palatine Hill, across the **Esquiline*** Hill, and beyond. It was the spring of 65 CE (Common Era), months after the great fire that had ravaged the city the previous July. It had burned for a week. Ten of the city's fourteen districts were hit hard, with many homes, shops, and temples destroyed. Thousands of people were homeless.

Construction was underway to not just restore Rome to her past glory, but to surpass it. The city would be safer, healthier (the newly built public baths were the best in the world), and better suited to be the capital of the world's most powerful empire.

*For pronunciations of words in **bold**, see page 46.

Before the fire, Nero had ended secret trials, given the senate more independence, stopped capital punishment, cut taxes, allowed slaves to sue cruel owners, given money to cities that suffered disasters, and supported art and sports.

"What do I have to do," Nero said to the stocky, fierce-looking man standing next to him, "to get them to understand?"

Nero blinked rapidly, as if trying to cover up his weak blue eyes. He was 27 years old and already had been emperor for almost 11 years. He had long fair hair arranged in curls. His freckled face, spotted from nasty teenage acne, was rimmed by a reddish beard. A white scarf was wrapped loosely around his fleshy neck. Years of no exercise, overeating, and excessive drinking had left him with a pot belly that his red-trimmed dining robe couldn't hide. Not that he cared. Why should he? He was the latest in a line of Roman emperors descending from Julius Caesar and **Augustus Caesar**.

He smelled as if he hadn't bathed in a week. The man standing next to him pretended not to notice. He had smelled worse from the emperor.

The man was **Gaius Ofonius Tigellinus**, the commander of the Praetorian Guard, a group of elite palace troops powerful enough to stir up the Roman people, choose emperors, and sometimes even kill them for the right price. He was also Nero's most trusted advisor even though he had come from the lowest ranks of Roman society. Many people regarded him as being closer to a criminal than to a military leader. A short sword hung from his belt. Scars on his arms and hands suggested he wasn't afraid to use it.

"The people are angry," Tigellinus said. "They don't see you as I see you."

"And how do you see me?"

"As a great leader and artist. In time, they will see the truth."

The setting sun turned the air around them a soft gold. Some would have found it beautiful. Nero was too angry to appreciate the sight. He threw the clay bowl containing the grapes to the limestone floor. It shattered on impact.

"Did I not sell grain so cheaply I almost gave it away?" Nero asked. "Did I not open my gardens so the people who lost their homes had some place to stay? Did I not build housing for them, at my expense, and order safer construction so that nothing like this ever happens again?"

"You did, my lord, but it doesn't matter."

Nero jabbed a finger at him. "Are you saying it doesn't matter that we now build more with concrete than wood to protect against fire, that the streets are wider so it will be more difficult for fire to spread, that buildings have porticoes for firefighting platforms, and that Rome will soon surpass any city on earth for architectural beauty?"

"That's what I'm saying," Tigellinus said.

"You're making me angry," Nero said harshly.

Nero had heard the rumors: that he had ordered men to pretend to be drunk and set the fire, that as the fire blazed he had jumped onto his palace's roof to play the lyre, that he wore harpist clothing and sang "The Taking (Destruction) of Troy"—although Romans thought it was more like "The Taking (Destruction) of Rome."[1]

In fact, Nero had been at the seaside town of **Antium** (modern-day Anzio), about 35 miles away, when the fire broke out. He had rushed back to direct the firefighting.

After the tragedy, Nero saw opportunity. He wanted to build a new Rome based on Greek and Egyptian culture. There were rumors that he wanted to rename the city Neronia. He spent huge amounts of money to build athletic facilities, theaters, and bath houses, so much money that the senate complained he was bankrupting the empire.

Nero also was building a new home, the Golden Palace. Many Romans were upset that so much land (about 300 acres) in the heart of the city was used for one man's luxury. The poet Martial had called it "An arrogant park which deprived the poor of their houses."[2] A

Legend, as shown in this 1897 illustration by M. de Lipman, had Nero playing a lyre while ancient Rome burned. The legend is wrong. Nero wasn't at Rome at the time, but rushed back to help save and rebuild the city.

joke at the time said, "Rome will become one huge palace, so migrate to **Veii** [10 miles away], citizens, until the palace reaches Veii, too."[3]

Nero ignored such comments. Didn't the emperor deserve a palace befitting of his power?

"You need someone to blame the fire on," Tigellinus said, "so the people will be angry at them and not you."

Nero peered over the darkening city. Who did the people despise more than him? Who would be the perfect scapegoat? And then it hit him. He smiled without mercy.

"I know just who to blame."

The Golden Palace

The Great Fire gave Nero the chance of a lifetime—to rebuild Rome in his image. The big project was his Golden Palace (**Domus Aurea** in Latin). The palace was laid out like a country estate with an artificial lake. Nero even built a 120-foot statue of himself as a sun god.

The state-of-the-art palace focused on the inside rather than the outside. That new thinking included a dining room with a revolving ceiling fitted with pipes to sprinkle guests with perfumes. Architects went with eight-sided rooms rather than the normal rectangular shape.

Art was everywhere. One fresco showed the myth of the birth of **Adonis**, the Greek god who represented the cycle of the seasons. It reflected Nero's passion for Greek art and culture.

The great Roman historian **Suetonius** wrote that the palace "Like a sea, was surrounded by buildings that resembled cities, and by a landscaped park with ploughed fields, vineyards, pastures and woods."[4]

The emperors who followed Nero built over much of the Golden House. **Vespasian** drained a nearby swamp and began building the great Flavian Amphitheatre, now known as the **Colosseum**.

Nero's Golden Palace, copper engraving by J. Blundell, 1770

Nero was only 14 when he became a Roman official under his uncle and stepfather, the emperor Claudius, and spoke to the Roman senate. Less than three years later, after Claudius's death, he became emperor.

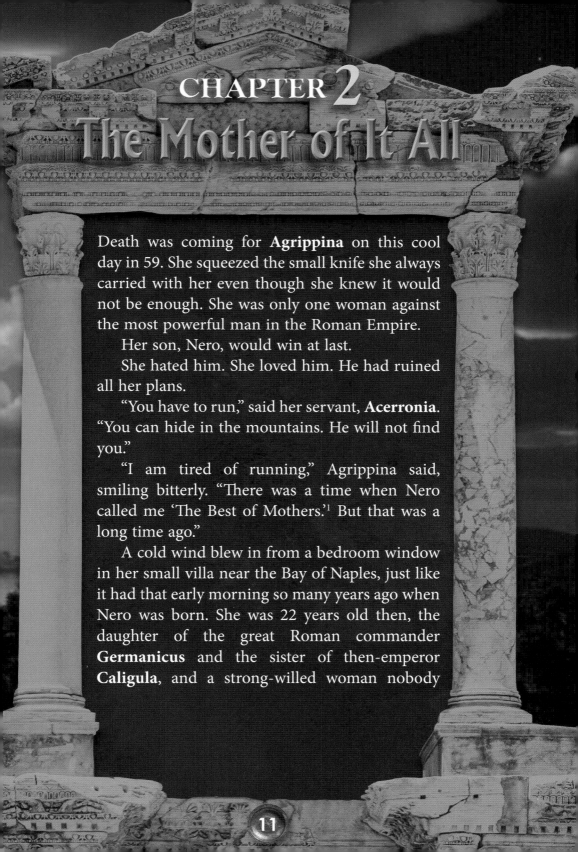

CHAPTER 2
The Mother of It All

Death was coming for **Agrippina** on this cool day in 59. She squeezed the small knife she always carried with her even though she knew it would not be enough. She was only one woman against the most powerful man in the Roman Empire.

Her son, Nero, would win at last.

She hated him. She loved him. He had ruined all her plans.

"You have to run," said her servant, **Acerronia**. "You can hide in the mountains. He will not find you."

"I am tired of running," Agrippina said, smiling bitterly. "There was a time when Nero called me 'The Best of Mothers.'[1] But that was a long time ago."

A cold wind blew in from a bedroom window in her small villa near the Bay of Naples, just like it had that early morning so many years ago when Nero was born. She was 22 years old then, the daughter of the great Roman commander **Germanicus** and the sister of then-emperor **Caligula**, and a strong-willed woman nobody messed with. Agrippina remembered the struggles of giving birth on that mid-December day of 37.

Her husband was **Gnaeus Domitius Ahenobarbus**. Ahenobarbus' bad temper was legendary. He once killed one of his freedmen (freed slaves), used horses to run over and kill a boy, and gouged out the eye of a man who publicly criticized him. When Nero was born, Ahenobarbus said that any child of his and Agrippina was likely to be "abominable" and a "public bane."[2] In other words, a nasty child.

They named their son **Lucius Domitius Ahenobarbus**. The little boy quickly suffered two shocks. Agrippina angered her brother, Caligula—regarded as one of Rome's most evil emperors—and he exiled her to the Pontian Islands off the coast of Italy when Nero was 2 years old. His father died the following year. His aunt, **Domitia**

Agrippina, the mother of Nero, crowns her son with a laurel wreath on his becoming emperor in 54 AD in this ancient artwork. He wears the armor and cloak of a commander. She carries a cornucopia (a cone-shaped horn overflowing with fruit and grain) to symbolize fortune and plenty. At the time, mother and son got along. That did not last. In 59 AD, Nero had her killed.

Lepida, took him in and provided education from two freed slaves—**Anicetus** (a dancer) and **Berillus** (a barber). When Caligula was killed in 41 and **Claudius** became emperor, Agrippina was allowed to return to Rome and take care of Nero. Agrippina had great plans for Nero—and for herself.

Agrippina became very friendly with the 60-year-old Claudius, who was her uncle. That angered Claudius' wife, **Messalina**. Messalina realized that Agrippina was trying to get Claudius to put Nero in line as the next emperor instead of **Britannicus**, her son with Claudius. Messalina sent assassins to kill the young Nero while he was taking a nap. But they were scared away by a snake that crawled out from under his pillow. Near the pillow Agrippina found a shed snake's skin. She put it into a gold bracelet that Nero wore for years on his right arm.[3]

She got a chance to get even closer to Claudius when the emperor discovered that Messalina was plotting to get rid of him and make one of her lovers the next emperor. So in 48, he had Messalina executed for treason. Agrippina married Claudius the following year.

She wanted to have her son tutored by the famous philosopher Seneca, who had been exiled. She convinced Claudius to allow Seneca to return and he taught Nero about philosophy, morals, the arts, speaking, law, and more. The boy also was guided by **Sextus Afranius Burrus**, the leader of the Praetorian Guard.

Claudius adopted Lucius in 50 CE and the boy took the name Nero Claudius Drusus Germanicus. A year later, Claudius designated Nero as his successor ahead of Britannicus, Claudius' natural son, who was three years younger than Nero. Claudius also introduced Nero officially into public life by naming him *princeps iuventutis* (leader of youth). Nero gave money to the people and the soldiers, led a drill of the Praetorian Guard, and thanked Claudius in the senate. He also became a kind of judge during the city's Latin Festival.

As part of her scheming, Agrippina decided that Nero should marry Octavia, Claudius' daughter. There was one problem—Octavia had a fiancé, **Lucius Silanus**. So Agrippina spread nasty rumors about him. Claudius believed them and ended the engagement. The marriage of Nero and Octavia took place in June, 53.

Finally, Agrippina was ready to get rid of Claudius. Late in 54, she made him one of his favorite dishes, mushrooms, then added poison. When Claudius didn't die immediately, a doctor stuck a poisoned feather down his throat to finish him off.

Nero became emperor and Agrippina figured she would rule Rome through him. She figured wrong. Nero began making his own decisions, often after talking with Seneca and Burrus, and Agrippina quickly lost control of Nero. He began having affairs with a freed woman, **Claudia Acte**, and then **Poppaea Sabina**, the beautiful wife of a friend, **Marcus Salvius Otho**. When Nero's wife, Octavia, complained, he exiled her.

Agrippina took Octavia's side. Nero stopped trusting her and removed her German guards. She started supporting Britannicus to become the next emperor. Nero responded by having Britannicus poisoned at a public dinner in 55. Realizing the danger, Agrippina cuddled up to Nero as if he was her boyfriend and not her son. Seneca and Burrus warned him about that and he forced her to leave the palace and move to the coast.

Three times after that Nero tried to poison his mother. Three times she survived because of the regular antidotes she took.

Now a banging on the outside door startled her. Acerronia ran to see what it was. She returned with a dinner invitation from Nero. Perhaps, Agrippina thought, her son had realized he had nothing to fear from her. Maybe she could return to his side. Maybe all her plans could come true, after all.

If she was careful.

"Don't trust him," Acerronia said. "It's a trap."

Agrippina slipped the knife under her toga. "He's not the only one who can set one," she said.

The Death of Agrippina

Nero thought he had the perfect plan to finally get rid of his mother. He invited her to dinner at his seaside villa. She would have to travel there in her own ship. While they ate, her ship would "accidentally" be hit by another ship. When she was ready to return home, Agrippina would have to take a ship Nero would provide. It was specially rigged, with a lead-filled roof over the cabin. When it dropped, it would crush anyone below and punch a gaping hole in the ship's hull.

The dinner went well. Nero served as the perfect son and host, while his sailors damaged Agrippina's ship. When the meal was over, she and Acerronia boarded Nero's ship for the trip home.

On the way back, the ceiling collapsed according to plan. But sturdy bed posts saved the women. The ship was sinking so they jumped overboard. Acerronia shouted for help. In the confusion, sailors thought Acerronia was Agrippina and clubbed her to death with an oar. Agrippina swam to safety.

Not for long. Nero sent soldiers to finish her off. Agrippina faced death bravely, telling them to "Smite my womb" that had given birth to Nero.[4]

The Shipwreck of Agrippina by Gustav Wertheimer (1847–1904)

This engraving shows Nero receiving the body of his mother, Agrippina. Killing her made the emperor even more unpopular than he already was.

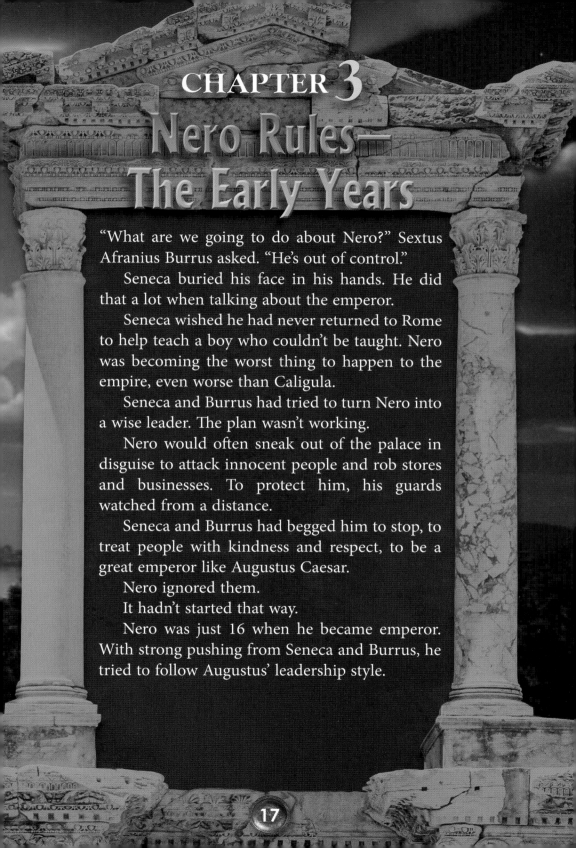

CHAPTER 3
Nero Rules— The Early Years

"What are we going to do about Nero?" Sextus Afranius Burrus asked. "He's out of control."

Seneca buried his face in his hands. He did that a lot when talking about the emperor.

Seneca wished he had never returned to Rome to help teach a boy who couldn't be taught. Nero was becoming the worst thing to happen to the empire, even worse than Caligula.

Seneca and Burrus had tried to turn Nero into a wise leader. The plan wasn't working.

Nero would often sneak out of the palace in disguise to attack innocent people and rob stores and businesses. To protect him, his guards watched from a distance.

Seneca and Burrus had begged him to stop, to treat people with kindness and respect, to be a great emperor like Augustus Caesar.

Nero ignored them.

It hadn't started that way.

Nero was just 16 when he became emperor. With strong pushing from Seneca and Burrus, he tried to follow Augustus' leadership style.

Did Nero really feel bad about having his mother killed, as this 1878 painting by John William Waterhouse, titled "The Remorse of the Emperor," suggests? Probably not. He didn't trust her and had grown tired of her plots and schemes. He was probably more upset that people found out he had her killed.

For a while, he was popular. Nero was respectful of the senate and gave it greater freedom. He passed laws to improve everyday life. He got rid of the death penalty and cut taxes. He encouraged new building projects and better construction methods. He reformed the treasury and ordered province governors to stop taking public money to pay for gladiator shows in Rome. He honored Claudius, the emperor he replaced. He was active in the courts and made fair decisions. He held exciting public games that included mock naval battles. He stopped the bloodshed in public contests such as gladiator shows. He even considered stopping the killing of condemned criminals in public events.

Nero was very upset that, when city prefect **Lucius Pedanius Secundus** was murdered by one of his slaves, he was forced by Roman law to kill all 400 of Secundus' slaves. Another time, when forced to sign the death warrant to execute a criminal, he said, "How I wish I had never learned to write!"[1]

Claudius did not want to be emperor. When Emperor Caligula was killed in 41 AD, Claudius tried to hide behind a curtain (shown here) in the palace. But a Praetorian Guard member found him and the Guard chose Claudius to lead the empire. He became the first emperor, but not the last, to be chosen by the military rather than the senate.

He was on his way to being a great leader.

And then it changed.

Nero got tired of his government duties. He became interested in horse racing, singing (even though his voice was weak and husky), acting, dancing, poetry, and, in general, doing what he wasn't supposed to do. Some called it "shameful and criminal deeds."[2]

Nero would throw parties from noon until midnight. Sometimes he partied in public at the Campus Martius (a large field outside of

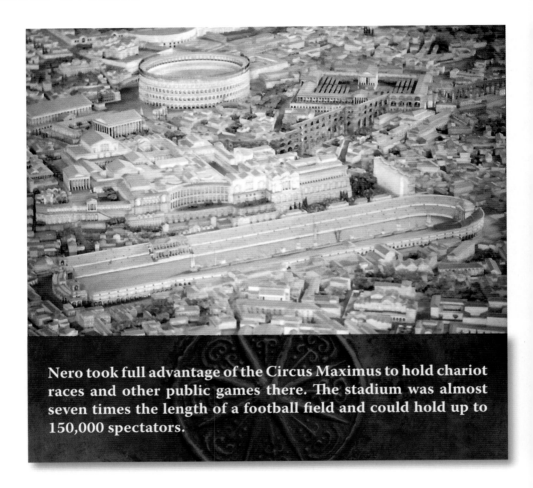

Nero took full advantage of the Circus Maximus to hold chariot races and other public games there. The stadium was almost seven times the length of a football field and could hold up to 150,000 spectators.

Rome) or the Circus Maximus (an arena used for chariot races and other public games), or he'd take boat trips down the Tiber River. The sides of the river would be lined with dancing girls, food and drink.

Still, because the government was running smoothly thanks to Seneca and Burrus, the senate and the Roman people put up with Nero.

But that was about to change.

The Life of Seneca

Seneca had a tough job—trying to teach Nero to be a good leader and person. In some ways he was successful. In the end, he wasn't.

Seneca lived from 4 BCE to 65 CE. He was a famous politician and writer. He wrote nine plays that dealt with Greek legends such as Hercules and **Oedipus**. They were so good they influenced the great English playwright William Shakespeare 1,500 years later. He also wrote 124 public sermons, called *Epistulae Morales* ("moral letters"), that ranged from being a vegetarian to being kind to slaves.

One of his most famous letters gave this message: "My advice in short: Treat your inferiors as you wish to be treated by your superiors."[3] He made the philosophy known as Stoicism very popular. Stoicism emphasized self-control and inner fortitude as a way of keeping often-destructive emotions in check. But he sometimes struggled to live up to those beliefs.

In 65, Nero believed Seneca was part of a plot to overthrow him, and forced his former teacher to commit suicide. He died by cutting several veins in his arms and legs and bleeding to death.

The Death of Seneca by Jacques-Louis David (1748–1825)

Nero did what no emperor had done before him or would do after him: act in public plays and performances. He thought of himself as a great performer. Few others did, although they were too scared of what he would do to them to tell him.

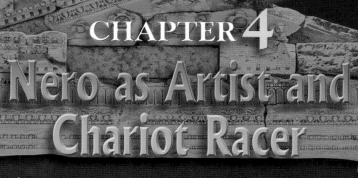

CHAPTER 4
Nero as Artist and Chariot Racer

The ground shook, the theater rocked, and then collapsed. People worried that more disaster was coming. Was this a sign the gods were angry?

Nero didn't care. He had come to **Neapolis** (now Naples) in 64 to publicly perform for the first time. In his mind at least, it had gone well. He had sung and played the lyre (a harp-like instrument), and the cheering had been all that he'd hoped for.

That no one would have dared NOT to cheer the emperor was a fact he didn't consider.

"The people love me," he said to **Epaphroditus**, his private secretary.

"If you say so, my lord," Epaphroditus mumbled.

"What did you say?" Nero asked.

"You are a great performer," Epaphroditus said loudly.

Nero smiled. Yes, an earthquake had destroyed the theater where he had just publicly performed. And, yes, some critics grumbled that Nero wasn't very good, but what did they know?

Still, the emperor paid about 5,000 young men to learn the **Alexandrian** styles of applause and to applaud "vigorously" whenever he sang or performed. These men were known for their thick hair and fine clothing.[1]

Nero liked to spend time in the city of Baiae, as depicted by Polish artist Jan Styka (1858–1925). Baiae overlooked the beautiful Bay of Naples and spectacular Mt. Vesuvius, a volcano that erupted and destroyed Pompeii 11 years after Nero's death in 68.

Just because Nero wasn't a very good actor didn't stop him from "winning" acting competitions. Very few judges would risk angering the emperor by picking someone else as the winner.

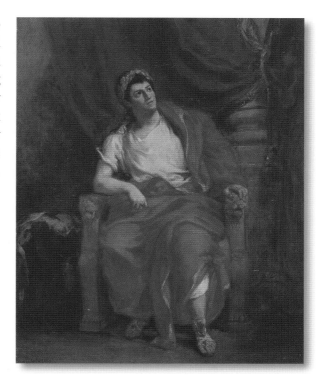

Nero would sing while playing the lyre. He would perform in Greek tragedies, plays in which the actors wore masks. This upset a lot of people because actors and musicians were looked down on, and public officials weren't supposed to publicly act or sing.

What made it worse was that no one could leave the theater when Nero was on stage, although nearly everyone wanted to depart because his performances were so bad and so long. Vespasian, the future emperor, was nearly killed after being caught sleeping during one performance. Some women gave birth during Nero's performances. Some men secretly jumped off walls to get out because the gates were locked. Others pretended to die so they could be carried out for burial.[2]

Nero would often enter into debate and speech contests, which were reserved for only the best speakers. To no one's surprise, he would win by a **unanimous** vote (the voters weren't stupid!).

Chariot racing was a brutal sport, which helped make it very popular. Races lasted seven laps and involved as many as 12 chariots, making it very dangerous. Drivers and horses were often injured or even killed as a result of accidents. Still, Nero liked to race chariots.

In 67 he went to Greece to participate in the Olympic Games. He competed in a 10-horse chariot race and was thrown to the ground. He got back in the chariot, but didn't finish the race. Still, the judges awarded him the victory. As a reward, he gave all the judges Roman citizenship and lots of money.

When Nero finally returned to Rome the following year, he arrived in a parade as if he were a victorious general. He rode in the same chariot that the great emperor Augustus Caesar once used. He wore a purple robe and a Greek cloak covered with stars, with an Olympic crown on his head. People showered him with ribbons, birds, and sweetmeats.

Nero had plans for other performances, but those never happened. The empire, and his ruling of it, was about to change.

Better Building

Under Nero, Roman architecture thrived. Vaults, arches, and domes became the norm as architects and engineers, through trial and error, learned how to make them.

An arch is made of wedge-shaped stone or brick blocks called arch-stones that stay in place because of the mutual pressure of one stone upon another. They are arranged on a curve to span an opening and to support the weight on top. To build an arch, a wood frame is used until the last stone, called a keystone, is in place.

A vault is a long arch covering a space. It's made of brick, concrete, stone or similar material. It depends on its components supporting each other under pressure.

A dome is a form of vault. The best example is the Pantheon, which is considered the perfect dome. Its diameter and height are both 140 feet.

Just as impressive was how fast and how well the Romans built. Nero's Golden Palace was built in four years. The Colosseum was built in ten. For comparison, some cathedrals in medieval Europe took centuries to design and build. Many Roman buildings from Nero's era have endured to the present day.

Even today visitors can see the beauty in Nero's Golden Palace, including a statue of a muse (an inspiring Greek or Roman spirit) in the nearly 2,000-year-old site.

Not everyone saw Nero as a bad emperor. In this 1561 painting by Bernardino Campi (1528–1591), Nero is depicted as a tough, impressive leader.

Nero dropped the messenger's letter with trembling hands. His face was pale. His eyes were moist. Everyone at the banquet hall went silent. They knew what was happening. Now, in the spring of 68, so did their emperor.

"All the armies have revolted," he said in a weak voice. "It is over."

Nero's fear turned to anger. His eyes hardened; his mood darkened. How did this happen? Who had done this to him? He wanted to blame the Christians, make them once again the scapegoats as he had with the Great Fire that had destroyed much of Rome nearly four years earlier. But as he looked around the table, he saw no one who would believe him.

He leapt to his feet, ripped up the letter, tipped over the banquet table, and flung his two favorite drinking cups to the ground. He got some poison, jammed it into a gold box, and ran outside.

"We have to go," he shouted to the guards. They shook their heads. They would not follow any more of his orders.

"Is it so dreadful a thing to die?"[1] one of them asked him.

While some blamed Nero for the Great Fire of Rome in 64, he blamed the Christians. He ordered some to be killed as human torches to light his frequent parties. Polish painter Henrky Siemiradzki

(1843–1902) depicted this brutal practice in his 1877 work, "The Torches of Nero."

Nero thought about leaving the country. Maybe the Parthians would take him or, perhaps, **Sulpicius Galba** of Spain. Galba hadn't yet abandoned his emperor. Nero could try giving a speech to the people and ask for forgiveness and another chance. Maybe the senate would let him spend the rest of his days in Egypt, but he was afraid that if he appeared before them, or anywhere in public, he would be torn to pieces.

He rushed to his room to rest. When he woke up at midnight, everyone was gone. They had taken his clothing and his poison, which he had wanted in case suicide was necessary. It was necessary now. He called for the gladiator Spiculus, hoping for a warrior's death, but no one answered.

"Have I neither friend nor foe?"[2] he asked, but there was no one to answer him.

He thought about how it had all gone wrong. He remembered the death of Burrus six years earlier, and the rumors that Nero had poisoned him to make way for Tigellinus. Tigellinus was, in many ways, as bad as Nero. He restarted the treason courts that had led to so many earlier executions. The courts allowed Tigellinus and Nero to kill anyone they believed were enemies. It all became too much for Seneca, who resigned. Nero killed so many people he saw as threats that his one-time teacher told him, "No matter how many you kill, you can't kill your successor."[3]

At about the same time that Burrus died, Nero divorced Octavia and had her executed. He married Poppaea Sabina and she gave him a daughter, Claudia Augusta. She was pregnant again when Nero, angry because she was complaining about him coming home late, kicked her to death.

During it all, Nero blew through money—his own and Rome's—as if it were water. He never wore the same outfit twice. He fished with a golden net. He never traveled with less than a thousand carriages, and had his mules wear silver shoes. He played games of dice, wagering huge sums of money on every point. He gave the gladiator

Spiculus and the lyre-player Menecrates land and houses normally given to conquering generals.

Then came the Great Fire. People blamed him for the fire and he decided to change their minds by blaming the Christians. Many Romans already were suspicious of Christians, believing they were involved in cannibalism and other bad things that Nero called "abominations." He made them the bad guys and some of the people, at least, believed his lie.

Nero put many Christians to death in public games. Some were killed by wild animals such as lions in the Circus Maximus. Others were burned as human torches to light up Nero's gardens. Later he executed two of Christianity's greatest leaders, Peter and Paul. Peter was crucified upside down and buried in what is now the Vatican.

In 65, Nero learned of the **Pisonian Conspiracy**, a plot to overthrow him. It was supposedly led by a wealthy Roman, **Gaius Calpurnius Piso**. Nineteen people, including Seneca, were either executed or forced to commit suicide. Nero had no proof of their guilt. He just got rid of anyone he suspected or didn't like.

In 66, a major revolt broke out in **Judea**. Nero sent Vespasian to put it down. Vespasian's containment of the rebellion set the stage for a bigger prize.

The Emperor Vespasian
by Peter Paul Rubens (1577–1640)

33

This 1897 Henryk Siemiradzki painting depicts another form of Nero's brutality toward Christians. Entitled "Christian Dirce," it is a re-enactment of the death of the mythological figure Dirce, who

was murdered by being tied to the horns of a bull. Nero substituted a Christian woman for Dirce.

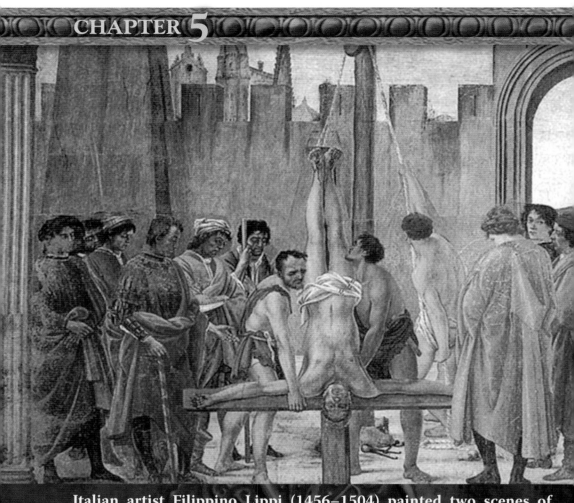

Italian artist Filippino Lippi (1456–1504) painted two scenes of Nero's persecution of Christians. This scene shows the upside-down crucifixion of St. Peter, the leader of the young church, Peter. Peter believed he was unworthy to be executed the way Jesus was, so he asked that he be crucified upside down. His request was granted.

When Nero went to Greece the following year, he left a freedman named Helius in charge. Things got worse. Many people were executed, including **Domitius Corbulo**, a victorious commander who secured the empire's eastern frontier. A food shortage erupted in Rome. Helius told Nero to get back fast.

When Nero returned in January of 68, he was in big trouble. He was so broke he stopped paying his soldiers and rewarding army veterans. Not surprisingly, they stopped supporting him. Desperate

One legend has the apostles Peter and Paul debating with the famous magician Simon Magus in front of Nero in this scene. Simon tried to prove his power to Nero by using magic to rise into the air. The prayers of Peter and Paul caused him to fall, and die. Nero put Peter and Paul in prison and eventually executed them.

for money, Nero stripped temples of their gold and treasures. He seized the property of wealthy Romans who had died.

In March, the governor of **Gallia**, **Gaius Julius Vindex**, broke from the emperor. His army was beaten by Roman legions and he committed suicide, but that set an ominous tone. North Africa leader **Clodius Macer** withdrew his allegiance to Nero. Sulpicius Galba, the governor of northern and eastern Spain, told the senate that he was available to run a new government if needed.

CHAPTER 5

The Praetorian Guard prefect, **Nymphidius Sabinus**, withdrew his support of Nero. The senate voted to execute the emperor. At the banquet, Nero got word the army had abandoned him.

Accompanied by three attendants, he fled Rome and hurried to the nearby villa of his freedman **Phaon**. He asked the men to dig a grave for him, weeping and crying "**Qualis artifex pereo!**" ("What an artist the world is losing!")[4] again and again.

One of Phaon's messengers arrived with a letter from the senate. It said he was to be executed by being stripped, tied up by his neck, and beaten to death. Nero didn't want anything to do with that. He took two daggers and tried to get the courage to kill himself.

In the distance Nero heard soldiers riding hard toward them. He thrust a dagger into his throat and collapsed to the floor. A centurion rushed in and put a cloak to the wound to try to stop the bleeding.

It didn't work. At the age of 31, to the relief of the empire, Nero was gone.

Nero's rule came to a violent end as shown in this 1888 painting by Russian artist Vasily Smirnov (1858–1890). Rather than die by a brutal execution, Nero killed himself. He was just 30 years old.

Rumor and Civil War

Nero's companions had promised that his body wouldn't be mutilated. He was cremated and his ashes were put in the Domitii family tomb near Rome's Campus Martius.

Many people ran about the city celebrating Nero's death, but for years afterward others put flowers on his tomb. There were myths that he wasn't dead, and someday would return. Over the years at least three men showed up claiming to be Nero. Many Christians would view Nero as an Antichrist mentioned in the Bible's Book of Revelation.

After Nero's death the empire fell into chaos. The senate named Sulpicius Galba, the governor of Spain, as the new emperor. He was killed a few months later.

Otho, the former governor of **Lusitania** and Poppaea Sabina's ex-husband, succeeded him. After a series of battles with **Vitellius**, the commander of armies in Germania, Otho killed himself and Vitellius became emperor.

Vitellius was challenged by Vespasian, who had come to Rome after his success in Judea. Vespasian's army was too strong and killed Vitellius in December of 69.

Vespasian took over, ending the Year of the Four Emperors.

CE

37 Nero is born in Antium, Italy, and named Lucius Domitius Ahenobarbus.

39 Lucius's mother Agrippina is sent into exile.

40 Lucius's father dies.

41 Agrippina returns from exile.

47 Lucius makes his first official public appearance.

49 Lucius's mother, Agrippina, marries emperor Claudius; Seneca begins teaching Lucius.

50 Lucius takes the name Nero.

53 Nero marries Octavia.

54 Claudius is poisoned by his wife Agrippina and Nero becomes emperor; Burrus joins Seneca as Nero's advisor.

59 Nero murders his mother.

62 Burrus dies and Seneca retires as Nero's tutor/advisor; Nero becomes almost impossible to handle and orders Octavia's execution.

64 Nero persecutes Christians after the Great Fire in Rome and begins building Domus Aurea palace.

65 Conspiracy against Nero by C. Calpurnius Piso is exposed and the plotters, among them Seneca and his nephew Lucan, are executed.

67 Nero competes in the Olympic Games.

68 With revolts blazing in Gaul, Spain, and Africa as well as among the Praetorian Guard in Rome, Nero flees and commits suicide.

BCE

146 Greece becomes a Roman province.

45 Julius Caesar is named Roman dictator for life; he is assassinated on the Ides of March the following year.

42 The Second Triumvirate of Mark Antony, Julius Caesar's grand-nephew Octavian, and Lepidus defeats Julius Caesar's assassins at the Battle of Philippi.

31 Octavian defeats Mark Antony at the Battle of Actium, making him the most powerful man in Rome.

27 Octavian is proclaimed Princeps by the Roman senate and receives the title of Augustus, which basically makes him emperor.

CE

4 Augustus's heirs, his grandsons Gaius and Lucius, die.

14 Augustus dies and Tiberius, the son of Augustus's wife Livia from her first marriage, becomes emperor.

23 The barracks of the Praetorian Guard are built.

26 Tiberius retires to Capri and leaves Rome to Sejanus, the Praetorian prefect; Sejanus rules so harshly he is overthrown and killed and Tiberius resumes power.

37 Caligula becomes emperor.

41 The Praetorians kill Caligula and make Caligula's uncle, Claudius, the new emperor; he favors the extension of Roman citizenship and permits the first provincials in the senate.

43 Rome invades Britain.

62 Earthquake damages towns of Pompeii and Herculaneum; Seneca reports death of 600 sheep due to poison gases.

66 The Jewish War begins; Vespasian and Titus lead the Romans and the conflict lasts for four years.

68–69 The Roman Empire faces its first crisis as four men succeed each other as emperor.

69 Vespasian rules as emperor and starts the Flavian dynasty.

79	The eruption of Mt. Vesuvius destroys Pompeii and Herculaneum; Titus, the elder son of Vespasian, becomes emperor after his father's death.
80	Construction of the Colosseum in Rome is completed.
98	Trajan becomes emperor.
101–106	Rome conquers new lands in Europe (Romania) and the Middle East (Jordan).
113–117	Rome conquers Armenia, Assyria and Mesopotamia (Iraq); Trajan dies and Hadrian succeeds him.
118–128	One of Rome's most notable structures, the Pantheon, is built.

CHAPTER NOTES

Chapter 1. An Angry Emperor
1. Dio Cassius: Nero and the Great Fire 64 CE. http://www.fordham.edu/halsall/ancient/diocassius-nero1.asp
2. Philip Matyszak, *The Sons of Caesar, Imperial Rome's First Dynasty* (London: Thames & Hudson, 2006), p. 261.
3. Nigel Rodgers, Dr. Hazel Dodge (consultant), *Ancient Rome* (London: Hermes House, Annes Publishing, 2006), p. 329.
4. Suetonius—The Lives of the 12 Caesars, Life of Nero, No. 31.1. http://penelope.uchicago.edu/Thayer/E/Roman/Texts/Suetonius/12Caesars/Nero*.html

Chapter 2. The Mother of It All
1. Alfred John Church and William Jackson Brodribb (translators), *The Annals of Tacitus*, Book 13.2. http://www.sacred-texts.com/cla/tac/
2. Suetonius—The Lives of the 12 Caesars, Life of Nero, No. 6.1. http://penelope.uchicago.edu/Thayer/E/Roman/Texts/Suetonius/12Caesars/Nero*.html

CHAPTER NOTES

3. Suetonius—The Lives of the 12 Caesars, Life of Nero, No. 6.3.
4. *Annals of Tacitus*, Book 14.8.

Chapter 3. Nero Rules—The Early Years
1. Suetonius—The Lives of the 12 Caesars, Life of Nero, No. 10.1. http://penelope.uchicago.edu/Thayer/E/Roman/Texts/Suetonius/12Caesars/Nero*.html
2. Suetonius—The Lives of the 12 Caesars, Life of Nero, No. 19.3.
3. Nigel Rodgers, Dr. Hazel Dodge (consultant), *Ancient Rome* (London: Hermes House, Annes Publishing, 2006), p. 54.

Chapter 4. Nero as Artist and Chariot Racer
1. Suetonius—The Lives of the 12 Caesars, Life of Nero, No. 20.3. http://penelope.uchicago.edu/Thayer/E/Roman/Texts/Suetonius/12Caesars/Nero*.html
2. Suetonius—The Lives of the 12 Caesars, Life of Nero, No. 23.2.

Chapter 5. The Fall of Nero
1. Suetonius—The Lives of the 12 Caesars, Life of Nero, No. 47.1. http://penelope.uchicago.edu/Thayer/E/Roman/Texts/Suetonius/12Caesars/Nero*.html
2. Suetonius—The Lives of the 12 Caesars, Life of Nero, No. 47.3.
3. Philip Matyszak, *The Sons of Caesar: Imperial Rome's First Dynasty* (London: Thames & Hudson, 2006), p 266.
4. Emperor Nero. http://www.mariamilani.com/ancient_rome/Emperor_Nero.htm

Books

Dargie, Richard. *Rich and Poor in Ancient Rome*. London: Arcturus Publishing, 2008.

Haywood, John. *The Romans*. Oxfordshire, England: Oxford University Press, 1994.

Kerrigan, Michael. *Romans (Ancients in their Own Words)*. Tarrystown, New York: Benchmark Books, 2010.

Macdonald, Fiona. *Ancient Rome*. Chicago: Reed Elseviere Inc., 2008.

Murrell, Deborah. *The Best Book of Ancient Rome*. Boston: Kingfisher Houghton Mifflin, 2005.

Whiting, Jim. *The Life and Times of Nero*. Hockessin, Delaware: Mitchell Lane, 2005.

Whittock, Martyn. *The Roman Empire*. New York: Peter Bedrich Books, 1996.

Works Consulted

Dando-Collins, Stephen. *Legions of Rome*. New York: Thomas Dunne Books, St. Martin's Press, 2010.

Editors, Time-Life Books. *Time Frame 400 BC–AD 200: Empires Ascendant*. Alexandria, Virginia: Time-Life Books, 1987.

Gabucci, Ada. *Rome*. Berkeley, California: University of California Press, 2005.

Gibbon, Edward. *The Decline and Fall of the Roman Empire*. New York: The Modern Library, Library of Congress, 2003.

Grant, Michael. *Nero*. New York: Dorset Press, 1970.

Griffin, Miriam T. *Nero—The End of a Dynasty*. Yale University Press, 1984. New Haven.

Matyszak, Philip. *The Sons of Caesar, Imperial Rome's First Dynasty*. London: Thames & Hudson, 2006.

Rodgers, Nigel. *Ancient Rome*. London: Hermes House, Annes Publishing, 2006.

Wild, Fiona (editor). *Rome* (Eyewitness Travel). London: Dorling Kindersley, 2006.

On the Internet

Emperor Nero
  http://www.mariamilani.com/ancient_rome/
  Emperor_Nero.htm
Emperor Nero
  http://www.thenagain.info/webchron/mediterranean/
  nero.html
Gill, N.S. "Nero Burning Rome," About.com Guide
  http://ancienthistory.about.com/od/nero/qt/012911-
  Nero-Burning-Rome.htm
Gill, N.S. Nero—Basics on the Final Julio-Claudian Emperor,
  About.com Guide
  http://ancienthistory.about.com/od/nero/g/Nero.htm
Owen, Jarus. "Ancient Poem Praises Murderous Roman
  Emperor Nero." LiveScience.com, August, 23, 2012.
  http://www.livescience.com/22650-ancient-poem-praises-
  nero-poppaea.html
Nero. Catholic Encyclopedia.
  http://www.newadvent.org/cathen/10752c.htm
Nero's attitude to religion and cults.
  http://www.mariamilani.com/ancient_rome/Nero%20
  religion%20cults.htm
Benario, Herbert W. (Nero (54-68 A.D.)
  http://www.roman-emperors.org/nero.htm
Nero murders his mother Agrippina
  http://www.mariamilani.com/ancient_rome/Nero%20
  murders%20agrippina.htm
"Seneca," The Roman Empire in the First Century, pbs.org
  http://www.pbs.org/empires/romans/empire/seneca.html
"The Life of Nero," Suetonius—The Lives of the 12 Caesars
  http://penelope.uchicago.edu/Thayer/E/Roman/Texts/
  Suetonius/12Caesars/Nero*.html
The Roman Empire in the First Century: Nero
  http://www.pbs.org/empires/romans/empire/nero.html
Tacitus. *The Works of Tacitus*. Translated by Alfred John
  Church and William Jackson Brodribb
  http://www.sacred-texts.com/cla/tac/

Acerronia (Ah-KER-ROHN-ee-ah)
Adonis (Ah-DON-is)
Agrippina (Ah-grah-PEE-nah)
Alexandrian (Alex-AND-reeh-an)
Anicetus (Ann-ih-CEE-tus)
Antium (ANN-tee-um)
Augustus Caesar (Ah-GUST-us CEE-zer)
Berillus (Ber-ILL-us)
Britannicus (Brit-ANN-ih-kus)
Caligula (KAH-lih-goo-lah)
Claudia Acte (KLOD-ee-ah AK-teh)
Claudius (KLOD-ee-us)
Clodius Macer (KLOH-dee-us MAY-kurh)
Colosseum (KOH-loh-SEE-um)
Domitia Lepida (Doh-ME-tee-ah Leh-PEE-dah)
Domitius Corbulo (Doh-ME-tee-us Kor-BU-loh)
Domus Aurea (Doh-MUS Ah-REE-ah)
Epaphroditus (Eh-PAH-froh-DIE-tus)
Epistulae Morales (Ih-PIS-chew-lay Moh-RAL-ihs)
Esquiline (Ess-QWE-lin)
Gaius Julius Vindex (GUY-us YUL-ee-us WIN-dex)
Gaius Ofonius Tigellinus (GUY-us Oh-foh-NEE-us Ty-JEL-neh-us)
Gallia (Gal-EE-uh)
Germanicus (Jer-MAN-ih-kus)
Gnaeus Domitius Ahenobarbus (NEY-us Doh-ME-tee-us Ah-en-oh-BAR-bus)

Judea (Jew-DAY-uh)
Lucius Domitius Ahenobarbus (Looh-CEE-us Doh-ME-tee-us Ah-en-oh-BAR-bus)
Lucius Pedanius Secundus (Looh-CEE-us Ped-ANN-ee-us Seh-KUHN-dus)
Lucius Silanus (Looh-CEE-us Sih-LAN-us)
Lusitania (Looh-seh-TAN-ee-ah)
Marcus Salvius Otho (Mar-KUS Sal-VEE-us OH-toh)
Messalina (Mess-ah-LEE-nah)
Neapolis (NEE-ap-oh-lus)
Nymphidius Sabinus (Nym-FID-ee-us Sah-BINH-us)
Oedipus (ED-ih-pus)
Phaon (FAH-ohn)
Pisonian Conspiracy (Pih-soh-NEE-an Kon-SPEER-ah-cee)
Poppaea Sabina (Pop-EY-ah Sah-BINH-ah)
Princeps iuventutis (Prin-SEP-us yul-WHEN-tooh-tis)
Qualis artifex pereo (QUA-lis art-ih-FEX pur-EE-oh)
Sextus Afranius Burrus (SEX-tus Af-RAHN-ee-us BERH-us)
Spiculus (SPIK-yul-us)
Suetonius (SOOH-tohn-ee-us)
Sulpicius Galba (Sul-PIK-ee-us GAL-bah)
Unanimous (U-nan-IH-mus)
Veii (WEE-ii)
Vespasian (Ves-PAY-cee-an)
Vitellius (Vy-TEL-lee-us)

abominable (uh-BAWM-uhn-uh-bull)—Detestable, loathsome; deserving of scorn or distrust.

architect (AHR-kuh-tekt)—One who designs and/or supervises the construction of buildings.

arch (ARCH)—A curved structural device on the upper edge of an opening or a support.

arrogant (AIR-uh-guhnt)—Overbearing, proud, haughty.

capital punishment (CAP-ih-tuhl PUHN-ish-mehnt)—Sentencing a person to death for a crime.

chariot (CHARE-ee-uht)—An ancient two-wheeled vehicle pulled by two or more horses, used in races and battles.

cremated (CREE-maytd)—Burned or incinerated a dead body so only ashes remain.

empire (EHM-pyr)—Large area consisting of many territories or countries and ruled by a single person.

freedmen (FREED-mehn)—Former slaves who have been granted their freedom.

gladiator (glaa-dee-A-tohr)—A professional fighter who engaged in public combat in ancient Rome.

lyre (LYR)—A stringed instrument of the harp family.

medieval (mee-dee-EE-vuhl)—Belonging to the Middle Ages.

menace (MEHN-uss)—A threat.

porticoes (POHR-tih-koze)—Porches or walkways with a roof supported by columns.

Praetorian Guard (prih-TAWR-ee-uhn GARD)—The soldiers who guarded Roman emperors and other leading officials.

prefect (pree-FEKT)—A high official.

scapegoat (SKAPE-gote)—One who bears the blame for the actions of others.

senate (SEHN-uht)—A legislative body of government.

Stoicism (STOH-uh-sizm)—The belief that people should live rationally and in harmony with nature.

treason (TREE-zun)—Disloyalty to or betrayal of one's country.